D0451365

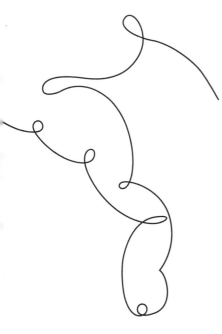

ADMISSION REQUIREMENTS

CALGARY PUBLIC LIBRARY

JAN   2018

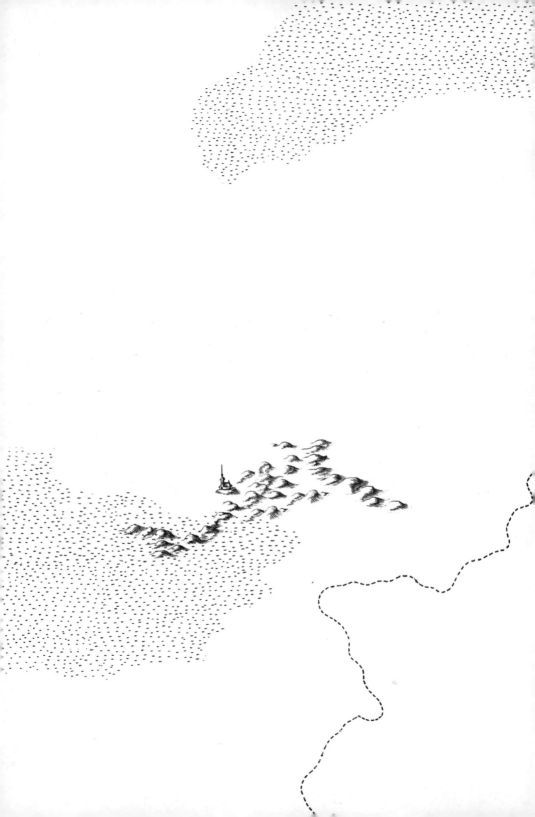

ADMISSION
REQUIREMENTS

poems

Phoebe Wang

McClelland & Stewart

Copyright © 2017 by Phoebe Wang

All rights reserved. The use of any part of this publication reproduced, transmitted in any form or by any means, electronic, mechanical, photocopying, recording, or otherwise, or stored in a retrieval system, without the prior written consent of the publisher – or, in case of photocopying or other reprographic copying, a licence from the Canadian Copyright Licensing Agency – is an infringement of the copyright law.

Library and Archives Canada Cataloguing in Publication

Wang, Phoebe, author
Admission requirements / Phoebe Wang.

Poems.
Issued also in electronic format.
ISBN 978-0-7710-0557-2 (paperback)

I. Title.

PS8645.A5327A64 2017   C811'.6   C2016-904524-2

Published simultaneously in the United States of America by McClelland & Stewart, a division of Penguin Random House Canada Limited, a Penguin Random House Company

Library of Congress Control Number is available upon request

ISBN: 978-0-7710-0557-2
ebook ISBN: 978-0-7710-0558-9

Typeset in Dante by M&S, Toronto
Book design: Jennifer Griffiths
Cover images: Public Domain images courtesy of the Rijksstudio, Rijksmuseum, Amsterdam
Printed and bound in the USA

McClelland & Stewart,
a division of Penguin Random House Canada Limited,
a Penguin Random House Company
www.penguinrandomhouse.ca

2 3 4 5   21 20 19 18 17

Penguin
Random
House

CONTENTS

I

II

I

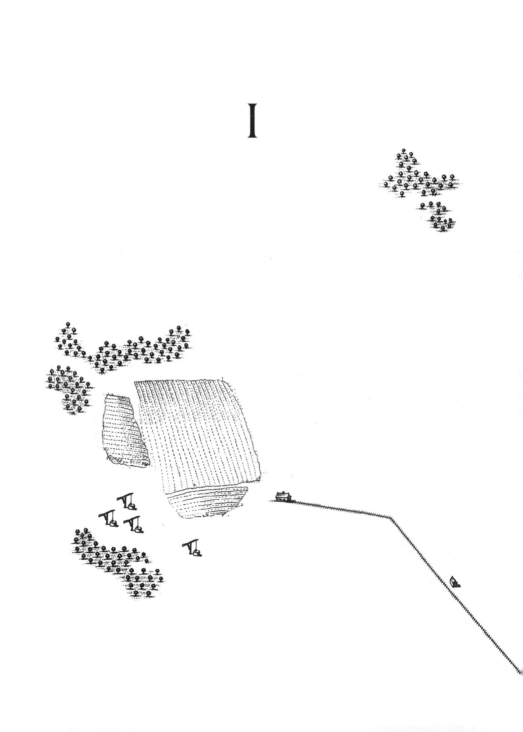

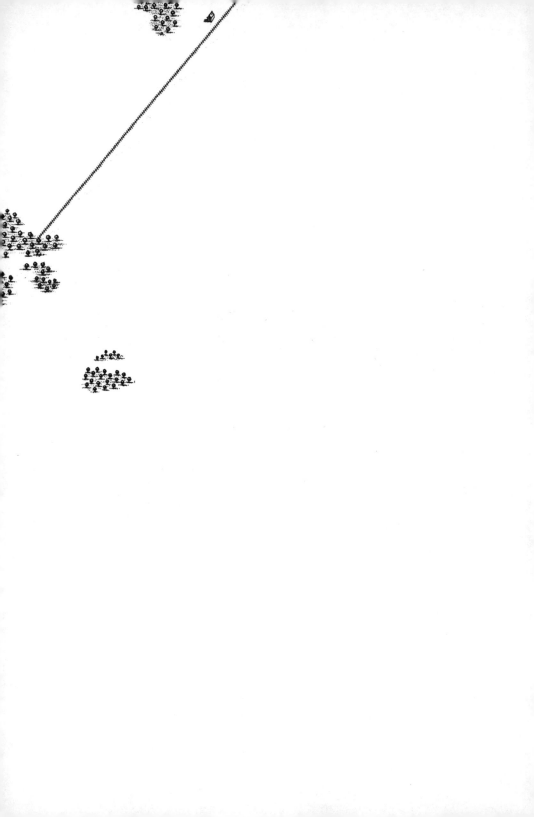

TEA GARDEN

Are we done at last
with the idea of breaking ground
now every bit of *terra nullius* has been subdued?

In the art of cultivating discipline, a grid conquers
that unruly yard, those previously landscaped
parterre beds so you can commence

scratching the crowded surface.
The messiest part of the business is behind you.
You don't have to bother

with stray, wildling pines, or dynamiting
resistant granite faces. Trails blazed by others
are guidelines. You can micromanage the dwarf trees,

the low-maintenance partitions buffering
your dry island. Think of how you'll displace
stalled sheds and fallow holdings.

Of what outcrops, bulks, and props you'll seize
to create a natural impression.
Think of where you'll invoke a lake

with white gravel, and whether rafts will float
across its quietude or if
you'll trek the long way around. To what ends.

Thousands tumbled overseas,
trunks packed in burlap.
On arrival they were in need
of immediate attention, fresh water, vitamins.
Could they make light of the punishing local conditions?
We observed them flailing like insecure tents,
hurricanes thinning limber crowns.
They publicized no sign of canker or affliction,
but inwardly were susceptible to
damp insinuations, and had to be rooted out.

♀

In spring the avenues blush at their good fortune.
I skip over the rail ties that shuttled women
to the canneries studding the Fraser's open throat.
At breaktime, the miso clouded over
with what can't be helped.
I won't keep these frailties,
not the thin-skinned blooms, clinging
to the tracks, nor the years I wasted on feeling
I had nothing worth recording.
I want them returned to me, pickled in brine.

♀

First signal your wish for a private moment.
Emphasize how slight the gesture, how it fails
to be more than a token of your fellow feeling.
Weather the patter of refusals as obdurately

as the rain's pestles hammering bowls
in bedrock. Even this gentle drama can erode
your resistance. Why the clogged, sodden
demurrals? You always meant to accept.
To dwell on your reciprocal gifts.

THE CHINESE GARDEN
Montreal Botanical Garden

Surfacing from the Métro, I consult
the map's lit arches and broken mounts
the way a fortune-teller browses an offered hand.

A passerby misreads my fate and asks, "Où est?"
"Désolée – moi aussi je suis juste arrivée . . ."

I wasn't always a stranger here.
These boulevards have seen the same brows,
dark as loam, the same profuse nature.

My mother hasn't forgotten she's brought me to this
garden before. She paid the price of admission

for her children. Inside, every example
is clearly labelled – Scotch pines tagged and shelved,
a flowering almond stuck with its formal name.

Tree peonies typecast ages ago by Marco Polo
as "roses the size of cabbages." Guides lead

straggling groups through the onion-bulb door,
symbolizing prosperity. Or is it longevity?
She took me by the hand and spelled out

what things mean. But not why lake stones
were prised up from unresisting beds and buried here,

or how to dismiss avid spirits to their rooms.
The lanterns switch on, a cacophony of rosy light.
I forgive them for outlasting the wire

and glue, the valiant tissue-paper hares and spheres
hand-cut by my grandfather when the luck waxed

to its peak and paraded for sale by his eldest
while every other kid in the village flew
grinning animals with inflamed tongues

and wan replicas of the fattened moon,
the old half traded for the new.

Please read all the instructions carefully before proceeding.
Use only permanent blue or black ink.
If you have special needs that require accommodation,
please explain.
The information you provide should not be limited
by the space allowed.
If you require more space, append another sheet of paper.
In the blanks below please provide us with the following:

your family name, your surname, your given names.
In the spaces provided below please list your middle name,
your married name, your maiden name.
        Please write your name exactly as it appears.
Do not neglect to include the names
of your clan, your forefathers, the name that is known
for miles around your ancestral home as synonymous
with a high-ridged nose, a scholarly bent, a particular
branch of expertise.
                        If more space is required, append
another sheet of standard-size paper.
Please print clearly the names your mother rehearsed
while you wriggled for leeway inside her.
In the blanks below,
                        fill in the schoolyard spit-ringed
slurs and concocted superhero monikers.
What handle foiled the forum's pingbacks?
Whose incognito initials bit into bark?
What property was signed away to the sand?
What petition was authored by indignation?
What name did you blurt in your sleep, the one

you never betrayed? What epithet couldn't fly
past the watchtower; couldn't be sounded
safely by patrols on night duty? Please release
your traceable aliases. Don't limit yourself
to the space provided. In the forms and voids
intended for this express purpose. Please give us details
that will identify you and facilitate this process.

I wake like a convalescent in an exemplary country
naked between cloudy IKEA sheets and a duvet
packed with goose feathers. I know a blanket
of snow has been pulled over the world

because I felt the weight of it like a benediction
as I slept, the air above my head charged and holy
by hands emerging from dark sleeves.
My furniture has sober, uncluttered lines,

and I drink out of porcelain. The food here
is milky – yogourt and muesli, chowders thick
with whitefish and biscuit. I stuff my mouth
with consonants and swallow trouble like salt

crystals. I begin to understand the basics,
Good morning, How are you, I'm doing well, Which way . . . ?
I buy a black coat as if I'm in mourning,
its high collar chic and vampiric. Until the day I die

I'll be in awe of the army of black bicycles obeying
rules of right of way, and strangers
with eyes like weak candles, who give me directions
to the bus depot, the licensing bureau, the quay.

The people have the look of kites being guided
by a sure hand. They dart and smile with little idea
of unspooling further, farther, kidnapped by wind.
The day is a suitcase and I've packed lightly.

THE JAPANESE GARDEN
Nitobe Memorial Garden

If you're still waiting
for your invitation, there's another
way in. If you find the gates of yellow cedar

swollen shut, apply again. Useless to argue
with the blatant crows. They can't be your escort
and still remain impartial. Don't bother

the box hedges, shapely and restrained, they've nothing
to do with your petitions. Send them on fiery
seeds like the tight-lipped sequoia,

pin them to needles of rain. Even the moss
can be a fist. If an asylum is your ultimate
ambition, there's a waiting room

screened off by bamboo where you can bide
by the custom – washing your hands
of indiscretions, humbling yourself before

the crawling-in entrance. Here within
the swaddled groves, the paper rooms, you'll find
the transparency you believed in. Every turn

of the cup has a prescribed meaning.
You know what it is now, and when to use
each implement placed at your disposal.

The landlord came over to ask after the six-paned
storm window, not observing

that my father had framed a bookcase with it,
made it the door to another kingdom.

He wasn't my dad yet, just a long-haired dropout in workboots.
I'd hear the story later about how his steel-toed foot

wedged open summer's tenancy while Mom grabbed
their nicked suitcases, maybe the same ones airlifted out

of Kai Tak airport a blustery day in February, 1971.
Samsonsite, paisley miniskirts, and four skinny brothers blithely

farewelling *Dai Je,* big sister. I don't know how long
I thought everyone had a movie cutting into regular

hours with tinted figures and pomelo trees
until I fathomed that every moving picture my parents

had packed was still unspooling across our plastered
ceilings and the dustless snowbanks of our surrogate city.

I didn't have to ask, *Where are we from?*
but I would have to answer it, again and again

like someone on trial. There's the short
version and the long-way-round version.

Useless to claim I, too, was nursed in this border hospital.
How I'd wished I had an envelope with the easy answer.

My skin presumed to speak for me of broken
threads. Every night our parents held the ends

together, but morning snatched away the family
compound, the ducklings underfoot, the covered-up well,

my aunt in her prep school pinafore, the anguish
of First Wife at my grandmother's rivalrous charms.

Questions dangled from me with loose
parachute strings. *What do you miss? What was it like?*

Monsoon rains visiting like a house guest, friendly shots
of firecrackers at New Year's, the whistling bobbies.

*My mother used to bang her head against
the wall to get her own way,* Dad said. *She was Second Wife,*

*the concubine, twenty years younger than my father. I never knew
her birthday. I never knew where she was from.* Adopted

by a Shanghainese tailor's family because it was thought
she'd make a lavish match, my *nai-nai* cut her threads,

attached herself like a clinging vine to my grandfather's
position, his spoken English, the factories where homespun

cloth was plunged in plain and came out
peacock-proud. *They never told us anything,*

my parents chorused. Every rumour a rope
tied in slip-knots. They gave us one end and let go

of the other. The only son of exiled
Chinese capitalists and the only daughter of old-school

Guangdong scholars in the Trudeau days,
the $2-an-hour days. There's no record of how many

instances my father passed that banner of black hair
on the stairs or if they whispered of all their future

rooms as the sleepless snow took the plunge
from his window to hers. Of what he proposed.

By June they were each other's islands.
Your ba-ba took a summer job in Gaspé while I did piecework

in a garment factory. They shifted houses like changing chords,
Chinatown rented rooms to college dormitories,

nomadic, packing up their LPs and macramé,
my mother tying one end around her waist and leaping

from a life entire. As if they'd been charred
to the ground, there's no whisper of the walls

containing the years. They were never our property.
They never saw our shrines, or ate our fruitful offerings.

Dawn's grey bars score
the windowsill where this pair's alighted
above the snow-slabbed park.
Their woeful murmurs mine the inner ear.
When have I gathered this story before?
During a season of shoring up a life
from leftovers, slivers, a clutch of straw.
What came after the displays
of courtship, the thwarted proposals,
after the veil of ice is withdrawn
from the panes? They are wintering over.
There's little to forage. The berries are gone.
There are still odds to be overcome.

Where did it come from, this fantasy
of shaping a life the way an axe
splits white pine into tinder?
Some of us were told a single story,
others, many. I thought it romantic,
those *filles du roi*, their trunks packed
for a life of linen sheets, hemmed by terror.
We've all heard about those people
who came here with nothing, well,
my mother was an unwanted
daughter too. I've been told on countless
occasions about my dad digging his way out
of shoulder-high snow in Waterloo,
shuttling cheese pizzas to University Avenue.
Did it drive them mad to listen
to the bitter wind kicking at the door again?
Not them – but us, when we first
came here and heard that howling,
that danger we've since forgotten.

The beach was a sheet of marbled paper,
wrapping up its initial offer.
Snow furrowed in mid-thought.
I'll hold out for something better.
Last night, wine-gutsy, we popped open
good news to share with a spread,
pulling apart the bread that'd been given
a slow rise, then knocked and punched into shape.
Before bed, I'd asked for directions,
and in the morning, followed their letter.
I've no idea how far I'm going, leaving everyone
back at the cottage, coerced into pairs
like snowshoe hares soon to shed paler selves.
It's not complicated. I find the path
to the shore like a foregone conclusion,
despite every obstruction in the way –
the mesh of trees, the bait-and-tackle shops,
summer rentals sealed up like unaired episodes.
I'd wanted to get my feet wet,
test the novel waters, but Erie's set
in its ways. Overnight, it has built a monument
to itself, both the maker and material,
raising an obstacle for the sake of overcoming.
A temporary country offering no hospitality,
having no host, nor even basic amenities.
I'd suit up and hike to Cleveland if I was
really ambitious. Up ahead is more of the same,
the shore meting out wooden markers,
leading me on with pier lights and criblights
decommissioned by dawn, gleaming ghostly

as missed opportunities. My path swerves
around keeled dinghies, stroller tires, debris
of a bounteous season, when we made waves
and waves worked toward the tideline
and the tideline aspired to its high water mark.
Over the peaks and valleys – see it?
Someone's left the stovelight on.

THE CARTOGRAPHER

If I were your biographer, I'd claim you've gone
farther than anyone could augur or follow.

I conjure you drawing in the margins
of your schoolbooks – spice caravans, camels, men made

of embroidery with black pepper beards. You begged
to peer through the incorruptible eye of Father's

telescope and at the other end you inspected big-
throated rivers roaring unintelligibly. I'm taking

liberties with your story. You bartered salt-flats
for another threshold. It wasn't built yet

so it cast no shadow, but you noted where a foot
had crushed the sage grass. Let's not speak

of dead reckonings. Had you imagined
what the rivers would levy, would you have turned

over every porcupine's quill and wolf's den
between Allumette and the bounties of the east?

Did you wait for an invitation? A moment
of your time. I just have a few additional questions.

What did the Wendat think of your tilted needles,
your ruffled sleeves? Who took you in?

I've been there, convinced I could pursue a more
convenient route. But you found the stands of white

spruce and balsam impeded progress,
so with snow stalking your heels and provisions running

short you took stock of what a life could settle.
No need to interpret the motions made

by the village elders, strict as a compass:
go back the way you came. You stood on their doorstep.

Disregard your maps, not because they bleed.
In every direction there are signs to the contrary.

SELF-PORTRAIT OF A DIASPORIC SUBJECT

The letters I send fly to their destinations.
Inside my cupboards are five varieties of rice:
Arborio, brown, basmati, jasmine-scented, wild.

I pocketed two white *azulejos* knocked loose
from the *praças* of Lisboa to tip the scales from weightlessness
to permanence. One day I'll send for the hope

chest my father dove-and-jointed when I was
eleven and volumes of Emilys and Annes travelled
with me in economy class. If my black duffle carry-on

was rifled, it didn't issue trouble. I carry the addresses
of other women who swapped glazed fathers
for advanced degrees in self-sovereignty.

I was born with bona fide blue stamps
on my brow that are coveted in thieves' markets.
The lineup I'm stuck in is moving faster than most.

THE CANADIAN EXHIBIT

That's not the way we do things here, I'm told
by the owner of a tea shop in Greenwich,
and I flush bright as a New World tomato.

I look right instead of left, backtrack over
Lanes and Ways and Courts, and marvel
at gabardined wine-imbibers displaying themselves

as specimens of *Contemporary City Dwellers*.
They are well within their rights to divert
the sun's rare smiles. It's not for me

to approve or disapprove of this city's obvious
hoarding tendencies. It's high time the Thames
coughs up the missing links and keys it's seized.

Only the most noteworthy finds
are tagged and numbered in a British museum,
or *the* British Museum, where admission is free

as long as you decamp with nothing
the law prevents you from restoring. These specimens
are accommodated by climate-controlled conditions.

Many-sided Roman dice and scattered
chessmen (whose berserk expressions have lost
their original intention) no longer tether fates to speculation –

the game's already played. We're all winners
of these ancestral treasures, poles crested with
gazes I can put a name to: raven, beaver, and mother bear,

but my connection isn't clear. In the shrouded
houses they once guarded, assembled kin recount
where they've been and what they've seen.

STILL LIFE WITH FALLEN FRUIT

after Mary Pratt's Jelly Shelf

The kind of light that gives itself away
by the handfuls, by armloads, for free, if only
we could keep it in stock. She had no plans –

her inspiration last-minute – a picnic,
a drive to the unresolved perimeter of the city, but in sight
of the familiar, the river, knocking at its receptacle.

"Let's go," she said, sending us scrambling
for whatever we needed. Dad on the hunt for binoculars,
camera batteries, my sister and I for diversions.

But she always had what she needed to take us beyond
the parking lot asphalt, the capsized chainlink
ringing scenic lookouts and the valley's assembled views.

We drank our fill of iced tea and years later, unsealed scraps –
a buttercup or four-leaf clover pressed flat
inside a sun-toasted paperback.

Each twirling far afield on maverick samara until
her call gathered us like returning boomerangs
when she spotted some roadside crop, sour fruits

of a government-tailored beautification project:
wild grapes, rosehips, and with uncontained glee
she stuffed every bag, box, and hastily wiped takeout

container while the rest of us indulged her,
finding reluctant pleasure in reaching
for a heavy, ripened load paid for

by a thorn's scratch and bite. Still, I couldn't help
looking over my shoulder for the permission
we didn't require, for the eyes that pierced

our backsides with questions never voiced:
Is any of this yours to take?
Rinsed, picked over, boiled down, and sealed

tight with barely a taste, the fruits of her labour
were more than what we'd come for,
and nothing gone to waste.

POSSESSION

Before we could see any progress,
my dad dislodged the blackberry vines,
I got the hooks from under my skin,
though the dark fruit was never within

reach again. My mother determined
what belonged and what didn't in the cold
drawers of the earth. We scratched
among its root cellar and jam-packed layers.

By spring the garden bequeathed us
with its prior arrangements. Roses gaped open
like the faces of coma patients,
tame and wordless. We couldn't spell out

the initials on the gate, or accuse whoever
splashed that aqua on the siding and trim.
The laundry line with its low-slung smile
wouldn't drop anything. When we prised

the glass from its blistered frame
it only denied, denied, denied.
But the loosened Formica was an account
of hard use and pots boiling over,

of hands whitened with flour, lard, and labour,
as if the shadow of the breadbox
and nickel canisters were still smeared
across the countertops by an oily sun.

It took two days to peel off the wall-to-wall,
to blast out the sticky spots with a thundering
industrial sand-drummer and the hired help
in harmony with it. Underneath were diamonds

of walnut inlay that hadn't felt the lash of light
in years. We smell blown candles in every room.
It's a kind of welcome, like a meal
slightly burnt. We suspect we're not alone.

HISTORICAL RE-ENACTMENT

Ram our attention down the ominous barrel,
tip in powder, ignite the weakened horizon.
Today no one's using live ammunition.

But the years have splintered open.
The day's heat-bleached, the sun's cowed
the grass into giving up.

Several of us invade the barracks,
but its cool cavern is already occupied
by a white-capped woman, doggedly pulling

at a piece of plain work she'll later unravel.
The smell is real, rubbed like polish
onto the barrels and berths – sweat, fear, and tallow.

It's another world inside the officers' quarters.
Since pieces of the green-sprigged serving
dishes are missing, we read

between the crevices of bone
china like we do the little looks not meant
for us. It's easy to forget

we're trespassers when for miles around
fields and orchards lie unlatched
and we've paid to be here

with someone else's long-gone peace,
the kind of deliverance that follows not
from victory but from knowing when to quit.

Cicadas sing their endless coda.
At the end of the day the actors cast off
their suffocating layers.

It doesn't feel right
to thank them. Even before this drama,
no one remained to defend our position.

THE QUARRY GARDEN

The scars still show – sumac's whip-marks,
red-gashed dogwood, elderberries dropping wet
on bandages of lichen and gravel.

While the day applies its grey balm to the old quarry,
cauterizing its veins, marshes are staunching
one site of the past century's surgery.

Blooms of ice seal in the pond, preserving
next season's plans under cling wrap.
There are still chasms to be filled in.

I don't ask for more than these dry specimens,
goldenrod, grasses with lionlike plumes.
They were hard to come by.

They were earned through collective effort.
Plaques of brick commemorate the reclaimed paths
like brooches pinned to time

capsules already looted and sold off.
There's no second prize
besides the mushrooms chewing on leftovers.

High on the ridge, volunteers in monkish orange
dress saplings in burlap and twine, patting them
down in cots of earth.

Night's anaesthetic takes effect.
The valley goes under, its reflexes slow.
We commit ourselves to its recovery wing.

WRECK BEACH

Our first impulse is to make our mark.
Chucked bottles and beer cans are spent casings
peppering the blast radius
of our firepits. We think since
kelp's slick clothing is already flung on the ashy sand
a little more or less won't matter.
The tide will keep drawing back its hand,
leaving behind what it can't carry,
not that there's much left here for the taking
except stones stopping the river's mouth.
We rifle the beach for foam pearls and the stuff
dream homes are made of, lived in, and then
set adrift like messages in a bottle.
Whatever we cast will come back to catch us.
And no matter how far we trudge
on the tide flats, that temporary country,
the rooms we covet remain cut off.

I'm in the midst of it. Bare feet interned
in dandelions, grass cuttings scenting my skin.

We sold the house above asking
but I'm still taking stock of our small plots,
the size of a family burial ground.

Though our bones would be foreign
objects in a valley famed for its amnesiac drifts,

sweet-veined maples, streets scrubbed clean,
arrowheads sitting aimlessly under glass.
I have exhumed the following:

        our secondhand push reel mower, rust-haltered,
        jars of tiger-eyed marbles I dropped

        like anchors under the house to be hauled up,
        and clothespins that bit dimples
        in our tank tops and flowered sheets.

Of course what I'm really looking for is all
of us, the way others comb for tribal scraps –

weft threads, or a toothy nail –
but we never registered our relics
in the alluvial clay. We only made shallow

> changes, my mother blocking out spaces
> on blue-gridded graph paper

> for her perennial favourites, each year rethinking
> the raised beds, though she never uprooted
> the crop of mushrooms, those rogue blooms.

As a girl, she had one garden she didn't share
with her bushel of brothers, tilled beyond

the reach of the template tides –
on the hilltop overlooking *National Geographic*
quality paddy fields and Discovery Bay.

> She nursed her escape
> on Beatles singles and *Life* magazines,

> until she launched herself, as if
> on pappus wings, innately aerodynamic,
> making her transatlantic touch-down

on an inclement constitution.
We were already colonial.

We would settle, we'd been settled,
and I'd tumble and spill over the conditionals,
the progressive past.

The growing season's short. My sister and I
between narrow beds turned each spring,

clinging to the spade edge of childhood.
We harassed the worker ants that built nothing
we could see, tenderly scraped graves

with Popsicle sticks for headstones,
sent fool's gold into the earth like packages,

pocket-sized treasure we never recovered.
My father's temper festered on sunken matter,
griefs surfacing as white-seared flumes.

None of us thought to unearth
those pushy spores, only cowed in our bedrooms

as Dad bit into poison, spat it out
before it steeped. He worked the mower
into the difficult corners. Its blades choked up,

he'd swear, then stall that line of thought
to unfetter the shiny reel from its onus.

Next he smoked out the wasps
nests and scattered past stings
before they burst from their white house,

from the playhouse of cardboard, held together
by games of *this is who you'll be,* of inviting

each other for tea, and the sheet tents
pitched over the laundry line with knitted blankets,
the rooms we folded up when no longer nomadic.

Refuges eluded my sister like strawberries
she couldn't spot. Every spring she was plagued

by microscopic traces, by strangers
who assumed she was a transplant.
Her face a sun flare, erupting to brilliance.

        I can't see her without turning my head.
        It was difficult to contain us in the same frame.

        Mom arranged us in matching Roots sweatshirts
        in front of the green tomatoes and other fruits
        that strained their supports.

She was familiar with the art of composition.
I don't blame her for showing us off,

but we were shy as squash blossoms abiding to the vine,
too closely monitored, turned adamantly
to reap the advantages of the sun.

        It was part of our early training,
        to look at the shape of things, though nothing

        ever keeps its shape.
        Our parents gave us the tools, the blank surfaces
        so we could capture pertinent details.

The way the light leaned away from the fence,
the fence that Dad built a door into

so the wands of our bodies could slip out
of our white-walled house and onto the mismatched,
mismanaged river flats. Yet we hardly used it.

When other kids were sent to their rooms,
we were called out of them like shy snails

to read the sky's auguries:
snowbirds scrawling cryptic codes in smoke,
hot air balloons blank as thought-bubbles,

forests of white willows and yellow
chrysanthemums that shoot up in an instant

beside the water and are chopped down
as soon as they lighted the contours
of our yawning faces.

One of us has gone missing.
Is it any wonder we flew

out of bounds, restless as clouds?
One of our chores was to haul in
the cotton pillowcases flapping

helplessly as flags to a country
whose capital recedes when we wake.

Only when I smelled the luck and clover
and the whiff of a thunderstorm did I guess
where it was, and how to find it.

Not by digging. Or paying green pennies like fares
into the past, or exhuming sealed

capsules left for others to extract. I let go
of my implements. Their edges sink,
have sunk, into rooms no longer spare.

SCOTCH BROOM

Given the chance,
who wouldn't do the same?
You rode in the coat pockets
of your forefathers, made your own bed.
Encouraged to spread
in all directions, you tapped deep,
rendered it a headache for anything else to settle.
We hold your success against you.
Each spring is a trial by fire. Yellow flags
highlight a cautionary tale.

JACK PINE

It's a skill to know the shape
the wild world has in mind for you.
You've hardly a moment to root before
your body's battered by the tempestuous years.
You're stunned to find yourself
alone. Your parents distant, fiery mobiles,
revolving in their crystal spheres,
your peers clinging to shallow sills
procuring footholds where it falls sheer.
You dream of mastering a certain direction, break
limbs, make trade-offs, bow
before necessity, and just when you feel
your heart tapped out, grow
into a grateful life.

INVASIVE CARP

Publicly, hourly,
the sun glowers in its assumed

role of crowd control,
dispersing onlookers toward

a stutter of stanchions next to
the surging lake.

Weighted gazes give chase
to the Bighead, wide-mouthed

kin of Leviathan suspended
for a count as immeasurable

as the heart, two beats, three;
caught on the sun's shallow

nets before wrestling free,
diving to the cloudy

bottom, stirring the bed
with its sickle-spiked belly.

Skeins of breath snag
on sticky fins. Shielded eyes

scan pilings and speedboat hulls
for its improbable return.

Someone's stopped dead
in their tracks by that baiting

stare, that come-hither dance,
and is hauled beyond

the harbour to sounder
waters, unrecovered.

As if fleeing disaster, we sprinted
up the salt-sloshed gangplank
minutes before they turned away fares

for the last ferry out.
My mother, my sister, and I spill hard
on the varnished seats, victims of laughter.

Like the deck of a Ouija board, the boat crawls
toward the outlying islands, keeping
intentions hidden, Lamma, Lantau,

Cheung Chau and Peng Chau, numerous
as the multitudes of cousins we were estranged from
but still fettered to.

The city is burning its birthday candles,
pink and yellow neon brand names
scrawling their best wishes on Victoria's harbour.

Across in Sham Shui Po, tenements don't fixate
on unprofitable passages they'll never make.
Up ahead, a manacle of light

chains the temple peaks to their fate, not visible
a half world away
where our blue beds wait for us

in the government town that keeps its canals
locked and quartered.
Summer and instead of piano lessons and pasta

we nibble coconut buns and listen
as Mom chatters about squeezing blowfish
with her brothers and collecting milk bread

from the docks to the family corner store where
customers scolded her for reading *Time*
magazine instead of becoming

someone's *tai-tai*, someone's
daughter-in-law. She's still bitter
the ferry's puttered off without her, but tonight

the tide snarled on our outstretched fingers.
We'll take it to bed with us, and wake
with the smell of dried prawns and incense

powdering the small of our backs.
At the other end, we let old ladies disembark
first, carts of onions and salt eggs jostling

down the ramp, then up the tapering streets.
The dark escorts us, and is our gauntlet.
Every night, we surrender

to those who've never left or thought to leave,
the prospect sinking unferried into the buoyant sea.
Every morning a narrow escape.

THE STONE GARDEN

Now there are only these chipped pills I can't swallow.
I used to have something to tend, some quick flame

I was convinced was colourfast but faltered
after the flash of infatuation. Well, that season's gone

like a sound mind. I've been bequeathed these forged organs,
these oracle bones already thrown in my favour.

If this is my home now, I must hammer out their rhythm.
But not yet. Because the first snow is shushing

the world, the gravel is repeating my footsteps,
and the courtyard is laying out its gameboard.

It's my move. I analyze my position from every angle,
as though every hour's a trial.

If only they weren't blocking my view. They are the view.
I crave instruction from those dumb tongues

on how to keep mum as monks, to budget
eternity, to grind light with wisdom teeth.

As if mass and compression were lessons
I could learn by heart. As if virtues could be modelled.

Around their shapes are shapes of other things I can't solve.
The stalemate of the day. The long con of the night.

ANOTHER VIEW

The evening's served on a blue-glazed platter
delivering itself with white gloves, soiled
by a smear of oil, or beeswax . . .

my window gleans from the parade of courses:
white moths folding like napkins,
dabbing at what the sun has spilled,

clouds opening their gates, crows clocking
by thick as captions. I read them
for further directions of what will take place

offstage, in the wings, where hours roll
like unused props. I go in search of them.
Across the alleyway is another

theatre, a full-blown production
sending the boxed herbs into a flutter
and behind them, the shadow-play

of love sitting down for dinner. The blinds
are lowered, but the scene lingers –
one of Ibsen's daughters

digs her nails on the wet counters,
calculates the distance between this day
and the next and the ever-after she's settling for.

CUSTOM DESIGN

after Frank Lloyd Wright's Living Room for the Francis W. Little House, 1912–1914

A skinny shelf above her bunk was all the room
    my mother had to store her treasured
        possessions, a barrette, a dozen colours

        grudgingly sharpened. A childhood shared
    with a riptide of brothers and cousins, hungry for a half,
a quarter, a sliver of adventure.

She customized a life, drew it to scale,
    unscrolled its blueprints and pencilled in details.
        The changes made were structural,

        deviating from the standard plan.
    To the unbuilt double-storey unit on its narrow lot,
she slashed partitions, knocked down doors.

The walls weren't up yet but she walked through them.
    She saw light making designs on parquet floors,
        and imagined how better days would show up

        against the white, pregnant paint.
    I was the shape of things to come.
There'd be room to show me how

to live with chimeras, that other family,
    how to bear their tongue-wagging company,
        how to sit for hours, shoulders hunched

as if against a phantom wind until they crawl
      foolishly out of closets to obey the commands
            of the eye, the line, and the emboldened hand.

STILL LIFE WITH DREAM INTERPRETATION
after Lu Shou Kun's (呂壽琨) Zhuangzi Is Free

What if

you never rose
above

the broad strokes framing your life?
But instead stuck fast to the pitch of your father's fury
that you and not your brothers succeeded

to his talents? It nearly happened.
The fine grind of gossip, the assembly line
work clinging to your fingers like pine soot,
the night-school English and the gaps it didn't fill.

No one gets it right on the first try.
With practice you'll be weightless
as an orphan, your own portable island.

Did you wrestle free of that dream
of flight or has flight shaken free of you?

II

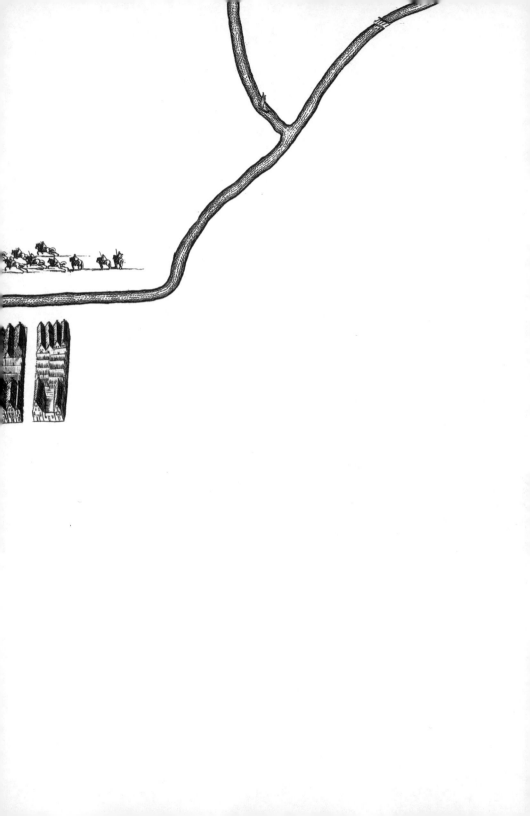

PORTAGE

i. Survey

If there's a lesson to be learned here
it's that you have to be
in the midst of it, waist-high in the Queen's
Anne lace, crabgrass, scrap metal,
and plaques of concrete, clambering over islands
of asphalt to set upon the river, lying quiet
after its century of use and abuse.
You have to go beyond townhouses
raised in the utilitarian '80s, cross streams
of mid-level bureaucrats surging down
Albert and Slater and Wellington.

I have things to settle here. Follow me:
this is the way to another province.
Be careful when crossing the Flats
not to trigger the snaking fuse of loss,
tangled up in the toxins of progress.
But first I need a few measurements.
They won't be accurate,
without Gunter's chain to convert
these empty fields into disposable units.
I count on a tripping stride, a restless foot.
The curtain of birch flaps open
to a cold rush, scummy banks, local facilities.
I ford a different water. It sweeps my body
downstream, as it has others before me.

ii. Display

We come early to find the best location
but are never early enough. Since yesterday,
campers and RVs slot themselves on the Flats
beneath the fleshless face of the cliffs.
On Victoria Island, a temporary encampment
without allegiances shakes out quilts
like battle flags, claims a territory of clover,
unpacks provisions. Kids with striped faces
thrash in the reeds and we call them savages.
We know the white-hot bouquets will
blow out in a moment, but still we accept
the giant chrysanthemums, the magenta stamens.
Our parents don't negotiate. They hand over
binoculars, straws afloat in root beer, popcorn.
The slate of the sky is marked with trails
I couldn't follow. My childhood dwindles
to a footpath under burnt-out streetlights,
between catcalls and charcoal smoke.
Amidst the clashing RVs from Aylmer and Wakefield,
my parents and my sister are spare as tea leaves,
towed away as I'm drawn into the heartbeat
of the night, hide drums pulsing, and through
the chinks between bodies in retreat, a wheel
of dancers from the Friendship Centre.
I lose sight of them, hindered by schoolkids bursting
spontaneously into the anthem. It's not possible
to sieve out the songs from night's collusion,
or the mangled stalks of loosestrife from the dust
from the tripping, stamping, backtracking feet.

iii. Developments

Along with campers, squatters, mice,
I slept atop fault lines that shook
slices of limestone like looseleaf
to land flat as bedsheets.
Chalk and sediment, those magnetic
stripes, record previous tenures –
comas of ice, an inner sea
where whales rolled like insomniacs.
A photo in a thin sleeve shows sky's
blue screen, a travelling matte
stretched behind hot air balloons barred
red, blue, green, hanging mobiles over
my mother, lifting my sister in the backyard.
In another, we're on location
with a picnic with takeout rice rolls
and *har gow*, a thermos of hot Earl Grey,
wobbly nosegays making their offerings
to the wind on its way westward.
We never caught another family
by the old paper plants, picking mica
between the rail ties, nor did we enlist guides.
I ask now – people of the river, Anishinaabeg,
how do I cede what was never mine?
How do we take no more than what we need?
A century ago, stove doors bounced,
brawls and foundries barraged the Flats all night
until fire swept it away in a losing hand.
But I didn't come here to write
about a vanishing.

iv. Barterings

The new owner entreated my mother to leave behind
the heavy, cream-coloured pleated curtains she'd sewn
to fit over the view of the brick-backed, modular rowhouses

behind us, and behind them, indistinctly, the Flats, and then
the many-named Kitcisìpi. No one could see into our lives,

so we'd rarely drawn them shut. My mother dug up
the white, empty-headed peonies but they took years to orient
themselves in a new, coastal city. I should've buried

something mythic, but ours were not the names
to be hand-lettered onto signposts or etched in loam.

Lachine, Gatineau, Rideau, and clay-leapt Lemieux.
Lebreton, Wright, and his farmhand Sparks, and Billings Bridge.
Our teacher shook free an aerial view: first-come,

first-serve patches on the English side of the river,
and slender, republican strips on the French.

But no one spelled the names of those who feed the spirits.
Our schoolbuses sped past the sacred places,
the chutes and shorelines we only knew as yoked by ring dams.

Let us turn to a page in our history books:
the river's toll-keepers, Tessouac's men, exacted payment
for passage through. What have we given up to be here?

v. Source

My father, and his before him, has a history
of absconding from points of origin
too muddied by churning undercurrents
to track down. As a boy, he'd run from home,
unlatching the dam gates.
In college he grew skinny, fed only by deluges.
At forty, his breath was sluggish, yellow-tipped
fingers holding my hand when we teetered
over the rail bridge west of the Flats,
the golden-brown water
swirling between the ties, its volume
turned low. My father's face placid
as the still creeks near Britannia,
our feet trackless on the backside
of shale and bedrock.
But how he raged at his lost birthright,
we pinching our eyes as if caught beneath
a waterfall, deafened by its concert.

vi. Founding Fathers

Qui va chap'tit, va loin. He who goes
gently, goes far. It was difficult country,
stands of white pine squeezing the way,
below, stomach-pitching foam. Single file
they dragged canoes along the brief shore,
not knowing the places of least resistance.
He was searching for a passage through.
Difficult is not the right word – civilizing.
Pour bien finir, il faut bien commencer.
Two centuries later, a farmboy trips
his hoe on a sunken astrolabe, its swinging
pointer coughing up soil. But its word
was never as good as the motions
of the river guides who didn't need to translate
their relative positions. Deposit your instruments
here, as payment for the other sea
the land held hostage. Perhaps he gauged
the price too dear, an exact science of measurement
trafficked for another kind of reckoning.

vii. Burdens

How much of a burden could it have been,
shared among a dozen
men, the canoe capping them like some beaked
clan animal? The burden of winter supplies.
The burden of being out of place.
And yet, if I stood at the riverbank, at first
I'd hear nothing
but waterfowl, swallows in the yellow tamarack,
then that concord, that hard tempo.
It was a backbreaking stretch
up the Grand Calumet, but there was no other way
around it but an old Algonquin route
that knew of shouldering burdens.
They bear the vessel that could bear them
over the outcrops, head first into basins,
where they couldn't hear their plunging intervals
above the clamour.

viii. Jam

Spring's an undiscovered country.
When we're in sight of it,
the city workers crawl over the ice-locked Rideau,
vested in caution, to cut keys
into the river's shut door, slipping caps
into the slots like red letters to detonate
a crisis. In the boom days,
logging crews sat tight, frayed, about to break,
waiting for winter to crash open like a safe stuck shut.
I imagine the sound to be like walls parting,
a house turned inside out. When we tiptoed down
from our rooms like amputees, Dad couldn't help
blurting, *For Godsake, stop acting like you're afraid of me!*
At slammed doors, I long to lie atop rapids
that can outrun change, lashed
to that promise of future returns.

ix. Lachine

It is one thing to speak your desires, another to name them.
I, too, was bent on being elsewhere
when bagging Florida mandarins with my mom on Somerset.

I, too, have a name I never use.
Ottawa, Odawa, a place of trade.
Bins of dried fish, flattened with fins curling up like parchment,

then the Yangtze restaurant where we'd order off the carts,
then a driver pulls beside me, mistaking my line of work
and I walked uneasily years afterwards.

What good are maps if nothing's to scale?
My father turning over a new leaf at the Plant Bath pool,
his slow crawl bringing him to the shallow end.

Afterwards, melon and chocolate gelato on Preston Street,
walking home past the yards with pocket patches
of reddening tomatoes, basil, sunflowers

turning their faces to inspect us from the porches.
Meanwhile the canal diverted the streets running east to west.
Water accompanies me. I take the long way round.

sit tight in painted pots, clearly labelled.
Various cedars, a Manchurian apricot.
A gingko spreads its yellow fans
shrouding mutinous thoughts.
When they've had a bad night,
there's no room to turn.
Some hand has been relentless,
breeding them to the ideal height.
Frustrated from their full-grown
shapes, their knots and boles
intimate potential.
To contemplate them is to feel
mushrooms and red squirrels
at your feet, to break free
of the highest canopy.

THE CHILD-BRIDE: A LETTER
after Li Po

I saw no changes in my life
those first years of marriage, negotiated
like a trade alliance. A child in a collar
of *point coupé*, I shivered beside you,
smelling of stale bread, already
greying from years of tribal wars.
In three months you were back at sea
sowing my dowry like a new kind of tree.

For two years there was little news.
I slept in my usual bed.
I was fifteen when you washed up.
I masqueraded in breeches, roamed Paris
for days, watching fine ladies descending
from crested carriages. Had I no thought,
my family chorused, of their honour?

At twenty I at last agreed to sail
from Honfleur. What can I say
about the crossing? The sea couldn't bear us.
So this was a new world: the raw smell
of lumber, of pig manure in straw . . .
At Québec the mud lay thick, the roofs leaked,
you were mortified. I watched you
kneeling in the rows of peas, seeing what you planted.
I spoke Algonquin almost as well as you. The women
didn't ask why I carried no children of my own.
Strange what I longed for most.
Not the cobblestone beneath my rose-ribboned

shoes, nor the crowds at the concert halls –
but the refrain of women's voices, speaking
like music my mother tongue. After
I returned, you wrote, *Madame*
de Champlain, you are greatly missed.

After you died, I gave up the world.
Did I ever write to you of St. Ursula,
who reached her fiancé in a day
by a miraculous storm? Some force
carried me toward you, then away again.
I couldn't wait.

We stood below with old parachutes
pulled taut as a seal's skin, sweaty palms
soiling the thin, worn silk that caught so many
small pairs of legs, girls hankering
for their first taste of death, even sour sons
whose lips unloosed no tenderness.
Some of us dismissed their flights of fancy.
Others bickered over trajectories,
or condemned the lack of direction entirely.
It couldn't be denied we'd been bluffing.
There were manuals for fever, for diaper rash,
for angels and anger management, not this.
The light we made scalded our eyes.
A breeze flicked the pages of their thoughts.
Some abided, hung in there, swelled and prospered.
But others launched themselves like ripe plums
to be wolfed down by the world.
When we caught them, our nerves
shook like vibrato, a note of consolation
that we couldn't hold long,
and we breathed in unison, a choir
made unanimous. Sometimes they thanked us.

We edged toward the lip of the clouds,
sizing up the shifting, still
wet canvases that catch the sun's curled shavings.

Who wouldn't tire of white undulating walls,
thin as seafoam? Not even the gods want the skies
as a home. Don't blame us.

It'd tempt anyone, the bracing and tidal
idea of travel. Also of arrival.
Most of all, we daydreamed of little things –

gates left unlatched, shelves to stock,
moths knocking like neighbours at screen doors,
our children with something solid

under their pillowed steps. We shipped out
location scouts to flip through the terrain –
the plains, the foothills, the mountain springs –

until they galloped like prototypal ponies
through the slot of our liquid eyes.
We tried our best to judge

distances, but only saw the veneer of things,
a topography dealt out like stoic cards
face up on the bright green baize, waiting

for our draw. Would it be that inscrutable valley,
with its blind mists? Or that delta locked in
by rivers latent as wicks,

ranged by peaks that looked like mere porch steps?
We read a founding myth in every quandary.
But finally we had to concern ourselves

with practicalities. Bylaws, bidding wars,
coltish investors. Let's not get into messy details.
Suffice to say we gave the order

for things to move forward of their own accord.
Antennae materialized in mid-air,
twitching like dowsing rods,

bridges suspended themselves,
construction cranes lowered their feet
into rain-logged mud, and condo towers dropped

downward, scales of rosy glass nudging the bottom.
We laid a grid of cherry-lined avenues and boulevards
like a net that caught their fins.

Trickier to fit together
the jigsaw of balconies and beachfront properties,
but we flipped over single-storey

homes until we saw the bigger picture.
We were pleased by how the city smoked and surged,
the streets steaming in the rain,

the crows that gathered at dusk like kids in sombre
uniforms. We glided down to start
our lives chugging like steam engines,

a bit nervous, naturally, at how far we had to fall.
We've finally clued in, when they came to fruition:
none of our wishes are in proportion.

It's hard to tell,
from this height, what's permanent,
what's a trick of the light.
Blots fuzzy as sunflare could be
ranch houses, granaries – ?
At this angle, nothing's upright.
Long-settled scores
total up the valley. Gradually I see
molten silver down the sides of the gullies,
the river, corralled by wide acres,
and a winning hand of soft wheat,
flax, sugar beets. The land had something
to hide and called our bluff, while we,
nested inside the plane's Matryoshka body,
wrapped in air like packing wool,
stake claims to narrowing quarters.
Whisked over those precious patches,
a little frayed, coming apart at the seams,
joined by concession roads and meridians,
my fellow passengers don't think
it's too much to ask for more
legroom, for upgrades, for sunlight
on our heads like a benediction, and yes,
please, as soon as possible, a better view
of where we're heading.

It's clear I'm walking into a cover-up,
white tarps thrown over the refuse,
the empties, the far-flung butts,

shopping carts with wheels spinning
in established ruts, coupled to their lots.
I crawled out of my shell only to fall

into a conch, diving for pearls of light
in a single breath. I won't go far before stumbling
on a soiled bundle delivered to a doorway,

flapping open to expose a figure without address.
He'll be sent on his way.
Scenic views are packed up and swaddled,

bridges suspended in utero, seawalls
bathed and dressed in diaphanous foam,
waiting in the world's intensive care unit

for a reboot. I can't recover the ground
I've gained. The day temporarily unavailable,
needing more time to heal: bruised arbutus,

banks mangled, fir tips severed from totem trunks.
When the sun rips off the dressings,
I still see pieces missing.

Across the city, you make advances
with sore soles, while silver-finned
trains sit high and dry
atop of tracks, bellies empty.
The news has been delivered.
Night's run aground.
Since streetlamps can't join the dots,
stars show the bigger picture,
announcing, *See here, we're ancient history.*
Disaster draws the neighbours
out like pale worms after a deluge.
Nothing shadows their doubts
since the moon shut its old strobe.
Candles give our rooms their notice.
I'll keep stitching and unstitching
each hour, digital faces sullen as oracles.
Without the articulate chimes and clicks,
or palliating hum of our energy
efficient appliances, I can finally hear
the spaces between us –
stairs protesting as if mistreated,
while behind our gallery of walls,
an audible trickle warns us
we're taking on water.
Something needs to be rescued.
Is it you, working through
the marooned vehicles while ordinary
citizens orchestrate chaos,
waving arms like batons? Later we'll say
everybody played a role.

No one lit them, yet they're burning,
dangerous as gas flames
if supervised. Clear notes
striking the same chord, rooted below
perfect intervals, minor and dusky,
unresolved. Surprising as the blue polish
at the tapered ends of your lover's fingers.
A bevy of cool blue-blooded Prussian ladies
with powdered hairdos teetering high
and wound with bluish ribbons, unswayed
by the riotous spring. But when the weather
revolts, they droop like fatigued lovers,
heads abandoned in the earth's soft trenches,
all their fruitless gifts already given.

We're a tenant of every hour.
The weather's adamant,
the earth packing its trunks.
Snow's pulling out its salt-speckled tablecloth
from front yards set with final offers.
Smudged clouds sweep the sky's ashtray.
Winter's outstayed its welcome,
though we aren't quite ready to shed
layers, to sign on to the liability
of perennial beds, crocuses, yearly
upkeep, power washes. We look forward
to the end of false starts, but weigh
our potential to repay the sun's
measured offers. The cold sets out
its terms and conditions,
last year's vines and wrought iron
curling like spirals of ink,
none of us willing to sign.

I'll look back on these days
the way I turn my shoulder toward
the tock-and-swish of the puck
along the boards during weeknight shinny
at the Dufferin rink. Winter's gone
into overtime. I owe you a visit,
last month's rent – while spring
storms want their due, rifling
sawed-off elms and green bins
for insurance we've stowed away
enough to weather a sudden downturn.
How is it creek beds have retreated
yet we still have trouble keeping heads
above water? In times of heavy volume,
when runoff and snowmelt exceed
the capacity of the system, know
your limits, the grace period before
you're frozen out.

On standby, recently revived,
couples on the gurney-wide sidewalk
are inductees into a life of shared risk.
They hold hands, towing each other
like freight cars the long way
        round a landslide.
Either I've taken a detour from guaranteed
investments, from lozenges of sunlight
on the backsplash sticky as spilled juice,
from complicities between co-signers –
or I'm moving toward the detached
and semi-detached, the power sale,
the bay-and-gable, toward the mismatched sets,
the pooled collections, the multipacks,
with fixed or varying rates of interest
in waking up in the free and clear,
the coin of blue sky paid in instalments
toward what we're owed.

There's a rent in the sky's grey parachute.
If I could turn its seams inside out,
hold them up to the light underwriting
our transactions, I might shake loose
our change the way overdrawn men
in the lineup at Tim Hortons disconcert
their pockets for what they can spare.
A recent census verifies the post-war
character of the neighbourhood, Victorian names
shucked from telephone poles like sun-crisp
posters of treasured family pets, lost and found.
Dover Court, Bellevue, Rusholme, our lives
never outgrew these red-brick villas, sylvan estates,
but contracted into self-contained suites.
Our tastes subdivided into compartments
like pastry cases, filled with burnt sugar,
pastels de nata, local specialties.
Some things we'll always afford.

CONVERSATION PIECES

The woman advertising her worldly goods
had already consigned her life to a city famed
for its bitter oranges, whereas I was in need
of a few key pieces. She'd accrued

a magpie's miscellany of water-ringed
teak and nicked cherry with qualities that appreciate
with time. I passed her what I owed in the lingering
autumn air. The cab driver eschewed

my attempts to help assure
the drop-leaves and Mission-style chairs.
He'd been here since '97, the same year
the birthplace of my parents reverted

to its former owners. He asked me
what the weather was like there, and I described
the big winds, islanders strapping down
their houses like passengers riding out turbulence.

We didn't have far to go. Letting myself in, I hugged
that awkward weight, pushing edges flush
against the blank wall to support
every mixed blessing I bring to bear.

PSA

It's hard to imagine the world could be
so far gone when the neighbours are doing their best

to keep their Highland terrier from ruining someone's
freshly painted exterior. Someone's sacrificing

his Saturday to deadheading spent perennials,
getting down on his hands and knees. White hydrangeas

nod their approval. They still think highly of themselves,
while boxes squat on the sidewalk and proffer old issues

of *Canadian Living, Cottage Life,* and *Farmer's Almanac;*
beside washed-out wide-mouthed quart jars ideal

for those one-dish weekday meals that are poured, reheated,
and served. Some woman yanks aside her kid the moment

before his pink lemonade Popsicle sticks
to someone's vintage messenger, the one with the treasured

patina money can't buy. Wild salmon's half off,
home-grown freestone peaches are now available

by the flat, basket or bushel, and the man ahead in line
has remembered, thank God, to toss

his reusable shopping bags into the trunk.
"Don't let Mommy see you do that," as his daughter finds

a stage atop paving stones. She'd like to be
the entertainment, not the entertained.

Forecasters predict another El Niño, and conditions
this winter will be near-normal, or below-normal,

depending on who you ask. Sorry to bring it up.
There are no public alerts in effect at the moment,

no cause for alarm. The satellites have our back,
and someone takes a break from his screenplay

long enough to look out the third-floor window
to watch a guy sorting through the bounty

of DVDs free for the taking. I'm looking forward
to streaming another season of that serial drama

full of fantasy elements but the lady next door warns
to prepare for the worst. It's already scripted,

which storylines will be forfeited, what likely
alliances will be conceived in a last-ditch campaign.

LATITUDE

"It's comforting to know that everyone is where they're supposed to be."

— *User testimonial*

You're the green light
in the palm of my hand.
I'm waiting for you to update,
to stammer across my dim display.
I've been tracking your progress
from playing fields to chalked-up
tarmac to empty lots. Best forget
the satellite on your shoulder,
your drone eye, your fly
on the wall, even if it's proof
you're loved, worth watching
like a jewel under glass
hardened by relentless pressure.
Danger surrounds you like weather.
Darling, nothing I do can keep you
from going off-track. Your life
is constantly refreshing.
Soon you'll be out of my range,
admitted places I can't follow:
secret clubhouses, gated
compounds, carpeted rooms
swiped open with a keyed-up smile.
For now I can foresee how far
you've left to rove.

THE PRE-EXISTING STRUCTURES

I've fled into the cool quiet at the heart
of the city, into courtyards unlocked
by maple keys. Here's an escape
from the glassy glare of the world, at least
momentarily. Here shadows aren't perturbed
by questions of their source and agency,
and I can stay to study the roots
of the ensconced oaks, or how to sway
the ivy while high-handed blackbirds bicker
in their administrative flutter and scramble
to elevated offices. I look for some great
design, and find only carillon regularity,
the sun shifting its weight from one side
to another. Others soon join me
in this sanctuary. We read into the hushed
tones of passing planes, parse clouds
and their pyramid schemes.
There's no end to the work I began alone
making meaning where there's none.

LOFT CONVERSIONS

WHEREAS authority was granted
by Council to designate the property
as being of cultural value and interest;
and . . . WHEREAS no notice
of objection was served
upon the Clerk of the municipality,
the council of the City HEREBY
ENACTS as follows . . .

    ♀

I'll find a new use for the summons,
for its gold-stamped notes already opened.
But the pear tree and its stooping head
have been given away, their dumb pendulums
gathered in. I should've broken in.
Rattled the chainlink, scavenged
the sinking traces, put it into storage,
packed up the hush in foam, sealed its edges.
I should've saved something.

    ♀

The architects have every intention
of preserving the integrity and beauty
of the original structure. The authentic
hard loft residences have been
creatively and sensitively designed
to capitalize on the grandeur
of the soaring cathedral ceilings and the rich

detailing of stone columns, capitals,
hammerhead wood trusses and majestic
gothic arches and windows.
Each residence is unique
from the rest. Experience it for yourself.
Register for your viewing today.

♀

Somewhere along Bloor, she lost faith
in the whole enterprise.
A one-woman wrecking crew,
she sent her message crashing through
with a patio chair from the Nova Era
Bakery. She laid her blame at everyone's door.
Displays caved in, something slipped
between the cracks of the Laundroworld,
the O Padrino snack bar, the Hasty Market,
whose owner, according to witnesses
outside the long-gone Paradise Theatre,
darted out like a bloodhound after a downed,
scattershot duck and caught
that limp thing, that frenzied life.

♀

Month after month, I see no progress.
Neighbours and I exchange significant
glances at gates padlocked like a diary
clasping patent secrets. Windows, blindfolded
with plywood, wait for the big reveal.
Meanwhile, the neighbourhood plays
a long game, papering over assumed fixtures

and hobbled ventures. Behind closed doors,
everything must go. Our days numbered.
We succumb to shifting demographics.
We're rebranding under new management.
Thank you for your patronage.

2

I do remit this building, and all objects
remaining in it, for any
lawful and reputable use,
according to the laws of this land.

This building, having now been
deconsecrated and secularized,
I declare to be no longer
     subject
            to my canonical
      jurisdiction . . .

CAREER PATH

Fully automated, multi-storeyed,
a paved paradise.

Haunt of the hushed-tone informant,
dealers, loiterers, and those lying

in wait. Scene of the hot pursuit.
Venue of familiar tropes.

A shell of a complex.
In plain sight, yet uncredited.

Among the rank-and-file who fill
every available position, you'll find a place.

The bar is raised. The slope is gradual.
You ensure you have adequate

headroom. Chevrons glowingly
exclaim their bias.

The path corkscrews higher.
Steer toward the top, where parked

in shadow are the vehicles of those
who drove themselves this far – Escorts, Explorers,

Civics, Silverados, Range Rovers, Alpha Rams.
Do you see your opportunity?

Signal your intentions after diagnosing
your blind spots.

Take note of your location,
the writing on the wall.

It's designed to bear the pressure
of the building's integrity,

its capacity for load-carrying limited
to localized failures.

You walk away for now,
secure in your convictions.

LESSON PLAN

Every day we build on the conversation.
They ask me the meaning
of the expression, and I tell them it's common.
I say, "Imagine you're *running behind*,
that there's somewhere you need to be
and you've *got to get a move on*. You grab a coffee
on the way like you grab hold of the unspecified things
getting away from you – that dredge of sweetness
at the bottom of the cup, the rearmost monarch
slipping summer's turnstile, your daughter's receding lisp – "
The whiteboard charts the model sentences,
the arched marks of inflection.
"Picture yourself *running into* an old friend,
whose turns of phrase and cool demeanour
bring back this very room with its rigid set-up and minute
hand suspended as if in judgment. *Let's grab lunch*,
he says, and you chime back, *We can get caught up*.
You're both *going places, hedging bets*,"
and in that moment I believe it too,
that if they just *hang in there*, they'll get
where they're going to in the long run,
in due course, as if my authority could slow
or hasten them toward the moment when
things don't need explanation.

FUTURE PROSPECTS

Under the myopic glass oculus
sealing the convocation hall, we arrange ourselves

in order, gowned in customary
Grecian robes pre-ordered, one size fits all.

This blown bubble, this porthole, allows a modicum
of what's accumulating over our heads,

ballooning out of hand, inflated column
inches totalling up to an amount we're already repaying.

While on the other side of the sky's split screen
is a view that maintains

its bluest confidence. In that version, the world
is presentable. It's shown up

on time. It handed in every assignment for credit.
Under its parentage, we proceed toward the raised area,

where we'll be acknowledged for our readiness
to audit and analyze its degrees of pressure.

Soon we'll fly out like canaries, but are we going in or out of
the coal mine, the dark pits our predecessors

dug for themselves? Until free to do otherwise,
we stay in our assigned order. Of course we try our best

to capture the moment, lingering beside
the donated wings, those picturesque arches,

before we disperse our brittle bubbles,
soon to burst, ranging for a suitable landing.

BEST BEHAVIOUR

I shared my answers. I finished everything
on my plate. I didn't speak
with my mouth full, or gesture
with my chopsticks while speaking,
or make contact if a stranger gestured obscenely.
With the covers over my head I only read as far
as the end of the next chapter, and the one after that.
I shared my answers. I waited my turn, to be
called on, in the wings. If some valued customer
stormed the counter, I deemed a fuss unworthy.
No real threat was posed. No one protested
at my behest for my fair share of *saudade*,
of the sidewalk, the prime-time hours,
the white poppies, the warm glass.
I held the door open as I left.

SWIMMING LESSONS

You always claimed it was me and not
our father who taught you

how to keep your head above the tinted water
and its chemical mix, even though each week

he took us to the pool where Vietnamese kids
thrashed like ring fighters. We raced

from one side to the other, Dad giving you
the head start because I was bigger

and didn't need his push. Afterwards
at the corner store he loaded us with treats

as if laying by credit for the rages
that shook him like a shadow puppet.

That summer with our grandmother
in Kowloon, I showed you how to float

on your back on the sun-planed shallow end
and we turned brown as Ovaltine. You provoked

Nai-Nai's ire, not finishing your meal,
and we witnessed a temper flying like a cluster shell,

embedding itself under skin, to burst
decades later. Week after week I count my laps,

thinking of the last dinner we spoke, of how you hurled
out from behind the bathroom door, tears hot

as fuses. An old dud is unexploded within
my chest. Maybe it's air you're drowning in.

STILL LIFE WITH SEA WATER, A LAKE, A FROZEN RIVER,
BATHWATER, AND A FOUNTAIN
after John Everett Millais's Ophelia

Because you want to keep your daughters
from drowning, you present them with opportunities

to know various quantities: rivers, oceans, lakes,
bathtubs, and pools that'll test their depths.

You play that Joni Mitchell song about teaching her feet
to fly, her claret-coloured voice wishing

for a river to skate away on. You tell them
about scrambling to higher ground, escaping

your duty-bound shift at the family corner store,
negotiating your release from the island that gave up

a few feet to the sea's bite every year
while tailors and butchers and schoolteachers hug

closer quarters. You let them accept
invitations to cottage country where they throw themselves

off floating docks, breaking the tension
with their wind-planed bodies. Let them shiver

in baking soda baths to pacify fevers until
they're clear of danger. You dampen your heels

in a green-tiled fountain, hand your daughters
each a wish to toss in. They review their options.

The milled edges fly, changing course mid-air,
but you don't wait to see if they land.

At any sign voices ricocheted and pairs of arms
hauled in logoed shirts and underthings like plunder.
But below and above us, lines were holding up
hundred-count cotton over our allotment of sky.

My grandmother looked out and gave the all-clear.
She made the metal curtains shudder and punched
buttons that governed the elevator down forty storeys
to the lobby, crackled as the shell of a turtle's back.

Armed with her shopping bag, she marched into air
so humid it had no room for protest and queued up
for commemorative coins with empty crowns.
She'd buy me golden McDonald's fries at the outdoor mall,

or multipacks of Kellogg's or Ovaltine hugged by
free gifts, uncalled for, uncoordinated –
once, a beach ball I tossed like a grenade at the tank
of goldfish. I was seven and tanned brown as cork,

blinking at toylike trams and red double-deckers
stuttering toward the noon-day gun soon to salute
the royal yachts and sandpipers in Causeway Bay.
When we'd barely advanced beyond the apartment

named for two queens, soft drops were bleeding
on my grandmother's speckled silk blouse.
She retreated to where my grandfather drowsed,
insensible, without a sound to spare for his only son

and many, untenable daughters. I was told to wait.
I waited for thunder, for clues that we'd be washed
away by the giant winds that wrap the island.
By the time her heels were rat-tat-tating

on the parquet, the rain was wiping its tears and the gassy
sun was steam-drying the awnings along Gloucester Road.
Still, Nai-Nai toted the umbrella, long as a sabre –
she liked to be prepared for sticky weather.

Since then, I've been hearing
the umbrellas opening and shutting and flying
and shutting and lining up against the wall.

First, our footprints.   This was to be expected.
They had no continuity.   They were hardly
more than a presumptuous wish, and could be
painlessly edited out.   Then our secondhand
sedan and the trellises wore cloying veils as if playing
hide-and-seek with us.   When they remained
cloaked as cold looks, we concluded they'd only been
lent to us, as if we couldn't be trusted to leave
an impression.   The avenue of crabapples forgot
my father had supported their rise to supremacy.
The pavement shuddered at the betrayal, but clutched
their white bribe. What of the tiny grocery store where
we nodded at Maggie's grandpa over his reserves
of longan and fresh peanuts? The impassive counters
we'd waited at, and been waited on? They lay
suppressed under a fine, sparkling glaze
commonplace as sugar, but otherwise spared.
Not so our timid smiles and frayed bones.
We didn't see them go.   That was merciful.
By morning, the Scottish terriers and German
shepherds who lapped at the hems of our clashing
woollen coats will circle the craters of silence,
making kind and wordless inquiries.
We'll fill in the cavities. We'll disavow the crimes.
As long as our routes recall our myriad ways.

VISITING RELATIVES

You always say we never go anywhere
so let me take you on a journey, a spiritual
journey of sorts – since I know you're constantly searching
for ways to improve yourself. You won't need
to bring anything, or pack anything.
I've already bought the necessary gifts, fruits in season, etc.,
and even though no one will expect anything of you
I'll teach you the proper greetings
on the way there, carried like bits of lint or dust
across the packed nucleus of the city and out the other side
where the butt-end of shipping centres
flaunt their dark mouths. We'll disembark
at the wind-kicked end of the line
and you'll bemoan that eyesore of a mall
and immortalize the graffiti tags legible
even through windows befuddled as a lake bottom.
I'll try to translate the neon characters
in the restaurant signs, which mostly contain
lucky numbers and lucky animals, as if referencing good
fortune would send it showering from clammed-up skies.
I feel I should warn you that when we arrive
at the waffle-coloured house, with its Legoland
trees and oversized garage, I might disappear
upstairs to help my cousin with his geography essay
and you won't know whether the big leather sofa
is for sitting on or just for display
since everyone's in the other living room
snacking on something in small bowls
even though in 20 mins we'll be piling into cars
and heading to one of those cavernous restaurants

where the cups are heavier or smoother or harder to hold
than the ones you're used to, and waiters don't ask
after your meal but glide up like robot vacuum cleaners
and when a distant relation asks about my job or my parents
I'll shout my answer for the benefit
of the old people wearing hearing aids like misshaped pearls
and my voice will drop and become richer
when I talk in a dialect neither of us learned
in schools but that I've picked up
the way a net picks up by-catch when dragged
along tattered coral beds. Of course I'll do my best
to explain all I'm able to
in advance because once we get there
my mouth will be full of small bones and slivers
of something aromatic that I don't know the name of
and won't get to taste again for however long
it'll take us to get here the next time.

Bringing the future into the present –
I insist it should be clear
what the participle's modifying, not to misplace
meaning or to leave it dangling.

The billboard's out of date.
The line already built, though I keep missing
my connection. A ten-year-old
asks if the world was always

in colour, and I say yes but we lacked
the means to capture light's crowded spectrum,
wavelengths of visible difference.
All he knows is grainy,

spent soil and farmhouses fading to white,
juxtaposed with jewel-toned
box stores, condos levelling up beside
the spiciest Szechuan north of the expressway.

Let's take a step back –
my accent's flat as these fields,
cadences scaling up the old bed
of glaciers that stalked off without a word.

It took me ages to get here. One minute
fitting my essays into narrow departmental slots,
the next driving home the take-aways,
the bigger picture. From the Old French *essai*

we get the sense of a trial, an attempt.
The wind's doing its best to make it
up to Newmarket by six. Each week, I show how
to make transitions. They follow my example.

The sea's distress call preceded it. Clipped
to a gull's yellow bill, delivered lackadaisically,
its urgency was diluted by distance.
But we intended to do what we could
in our depreciated power. Knowing it would
be parched, apoplectic, we collected ourselves.
We stockpiled a surfeit of blankets and goodwill.
But when the first wave of storm-worn faces
engulfed us, shorn of its silver hoard,
willow-ware, and coral plazas, we'll admit
we were put off. Its eyes were empire-hunted.
Its thirsty queues wreathed our villages
like tattered scarves. We dispensed makeshift
comfort until our legs didn't want to be our
legs any longer, couldn't rest in their easy berths.
And still the tide's high horses stampeded
through our ports and pastel squares and out
the other side. It hung its knotted hair to dry
in our orchards and flooded our front yards
with saline afflictions. We tried to sweep it
from our stoops, but it slipped in like a note
under the door. It repatriated our pearl necklaces,
sponsored our spare rooms. Amassed a capital
of seaglass and ghost nets, traded in
second winds. When ranks of selkie children filed
into our brick-red institutions, we schooled
each of them on the capacities, volumes,
and formulas that equate the human.

by the millions as if homing
for a country we'd never discovered
but once believed existed. We left live
cultures to sour, costumes to moulder.
Degrees went unmastered, guides for self
improvement were stacked against us,
their backs broken. We gave up
our achievements like shredded sails
that once propelled us on our committed tack.
We forgot combinations, dispensed with
damage deposits. Dates to compulsory tests
bypassed us like express trains rattling
recent vacancies. Cities conducted business
as usual – but grime left wishful fingerprints
at high-rise facades, newsstands kept their lids shut,
coats at the cleaners were unimpressed.
Though ceilings were broken, dues were paid,
no one asked after us in our endless queues
by the sea that didn't hold its breath.
Harbours were restocked with scenes
from old films, paintings slick with oil –
passengers shuttled back to requisitioned ships,
papers forgot their order, scarves ceased their flutter.
The new world faded like a tattoo foolishly
published. Behind us coastlines wavered,
bars of land dissolving until
our slurred names peeled off like wild geese,
circling back to where they came from.

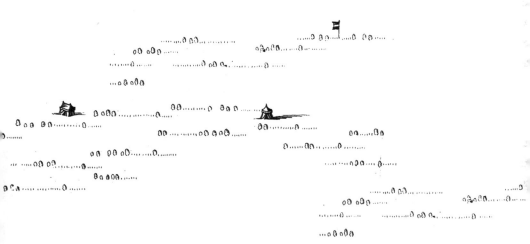

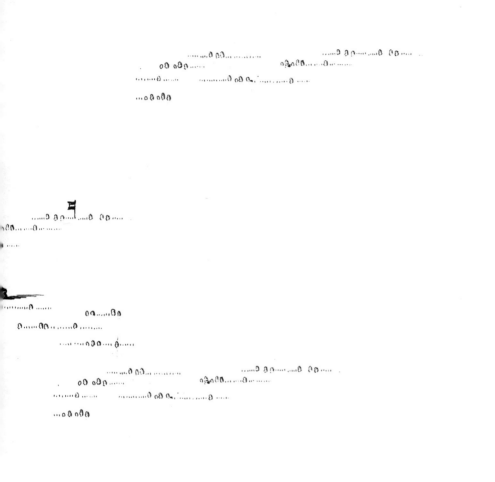

"Tea Garden" and "The Japanese Garden" use material found on the University of British Columbia's Botanical Gardens website.

"Historical Re-enactment" is situated in Fort George National Historical Site, Niagara-on-the-Lake, Ontario.

"The Quarry Garden" makes reference to the Evergreen Brick Works' Lower Don Project.

"Portage" and "The Cartographer" draw from Phil Jenkins's *An Acre of Time* (Toronto: MacFarlane Walter & Ross, 1996; reissued by Chelsea Books, 2008); and David Hackett Fischer's *Champlain's Dream* (Toronto: Knopf Canada, 2008).

"Loft Conversions" makes use of found material from *Reasons for Designation - 40 Westmoreland Avenue*, Toronto City Council, Heritage Preservation Services, 2007; Dog Day Developers website, "West40 Residences"; and *The Book of Occasional Services* (New York: Church Publishing, 2004).

"I Hear It's Raining" is dedicated to the student protestors of Hong Kong's Umbrella Revolution, a series of sit-in protests that took place from September to December 2014.

The opening line of "Regional Transit" is from a York Region Transit/ Viva billboard next to Highway 7 and Bayview Avenue.

ACKNOWLEDGEMENTS

Thank you to the editors of *Arc Poetry Magazine, BafterC, Canada and Beyond, Canadian Literature, Contemporary Verse 2, Geist, Hamilton Arts & Letters, The Hart House Review, The Malahat Review, Maissoneuve, Prism international, Poetry is Dead, Ricepaper Magazine, The Rusty Toque,* and *THIS Magazine,* who published earlier versions of these poems.

Thank you to the Toronto Arts Council, Ontario Arts Council, and Canada Council for vital financial support during the writing of these poems.

Much gratitude to my editor, Dionne Brand, for passion and for "burnishing." I cannot thank enough Anita Chong, Heather Sangster, and the McClelland & Stewart dream-maker machinery. Thanks to Jennifer Griffiths for my cover, and to Ken Babstock for bringing me in from the cold.

Thank you to Andrew Faulker and Leigh Nash at The Emergency Response Unit for energy and edits on my chapbook, *Hanging Exhibits.*

Thank you to the Canterbury High School Literary Arts Program. Thank you to Diaspora Dialogues; to Jan Zwicky for early support and sightlines and to the Banff Centre for Arts and Creativity; and to Denise Duhamel and the staff of the Disquiet International Literary Program.

To Rosemary Sullivan and the Group of Seven, thanks for believing. Heartfelt thanks to my mentor, Al Moritz, who always saw a book.

Raised glasses to Bardia Sinaee, Laura Clarke, Catriona Wright, Ted Nolan, Michael Prior, Vincent Colistro, and Michelle Brown. Daniel Renton, I owe you something.

For inspiring friendships, thank you to Emily Cook, Larissa Momryk, Joanne Leow, Amanda Thambirajah, Souvankham Thammavongsa, Janada Hawthorne de Silva, and Sandra Pozcobut. Thank you to Shawn Reynar for being my inconstant constant.

This book is dedicated to my family and my hungry ancestors.

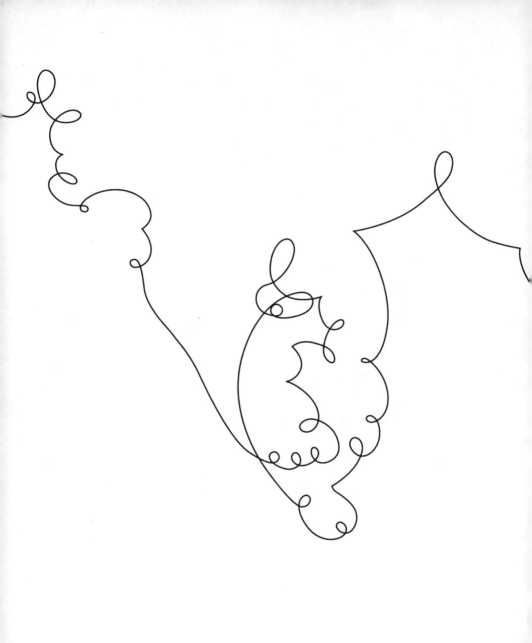